SHW

ALLEN COUNTY PUBLIC LIBRARY

3 1833 04~~75 4~~28

APR 0 6 2006

D1010433

Lexile: BR
U ☑yes ☐no
SJ ☐yes ☐no
BL: .6
Pts: .5

Written by Dawn Anderson
Illustrated by Kelley Cunningham

Children's Press®
A Division of Scholastic Inc.
New York • Toronto • London • Auckland • Sydney
Mexico City • New Delhi • Hong Kong
Danbury, Connecticut

Allen County Public Library

To my parents Donald and Dolores,
and to my husband Michael
—D.A.

For my sons Sam, Noah, and Nathaniel
—K.C.

Reading Consultant

Eileen Robinson
Reading Specialist

Library of Congress Cataloging-in-Publication Data

Anderson, Dawn, 1977-
 I am the artist! / written by Dawn Anderson ; illustrated by Kelley Cunningham.
    p. cm. — (A rookie reader)
 Summary: A young boy has fun creating a painting with a variety of colors.
 ISBN 0-516-24976-2 (lib. bdg.)   0-516-24912-6 (pbk.)
 [1. Painting—Fiction. 2. Color—Fiction.] I. Cunningham, Kelley, 1963- ill. II. Title. III. Series.
 PZ7.A533124Iaam 2006
 [E]—dc22
                                2005016128

© 2006 by Scholastic Inc.
Illlustrations © 2006 by Kelley Cunningham
All rights reserved. Published simultaneously in Canada.
Printed in Mexico.

CHILDREN'S PRESS, and A ROOKIE READER®, and associated logos are trademarks and/or
registered trademarks of Scholastic Library Publishing. SCHOLASTIC and associated logos
are trademarks and/or registered trademarks of Scholastic Inc.
1 2 3 4 5 6 7 8 9 10 R 15 14 13 12 11 10 09 08 07 06

My little sister paints.

I think it's silly.
She gets all messy.

Paint is in her hair
and on the cat!

She looks like she
is having fun.

Maybe I'll give it a try.
I pick up a brush.

I paint a sky.
I make it blue.

13

I paint a sun.
I make it yellow.

I paint a cloud.
I make it white.

17

I paint a tree.
I make it green.

19

I paint an apple.
I make it red.

21

I paint a rock.
I make it brown.

I paint a flower.
I make it orange.

I paint a lion.
I make it purple.

"Lions aren't purple!"
says my sister.

"I am the artist!" I say.

31

Word List (58 Words)

(Words in **bold** are story words that are repeated throughout the text.

a
all
am
an
and
apple
aren't
artist
blue
brown
brush
cat
cloud
flower
fun
gets
give
green
hair
having

her
I
I'll
in
is
it
it's
like
lion
lions
little
looks
make
maybe
messy
my
on
orange
paint
paints

pick
purple
red
rock
say
says
she
silly
sister
sky
sun
the
think
tree
try
up
white
yellow

About the Author

Dawn Anderson has been writing stories since she was a young girl. She lives in Overland Park, Kansas, with her husband, Mike, their dog, and two cats. When she is not writing stories, Dawn likes to be an artist herself.

About the Illustrator

Kelley Cunningham always wanted to be an artist and began drawing when she was a young girl. She's very happy to be getting paid to do something she loves. Born in Wisconsin, Kelley now lives in New Jersey with her husband and three sons.